10 Money Skills For Teenagers

Your Superpower To Create Wealth

Elizabeth E James

EMA Publishing

This publication is designed to provide accurate and authoritative information in regard to the subject matter covered. It is sold with the understanding that neither the author nor the publisher is engaged in rendering legal, investment, accounting or other professional services. While the publisher and author have used their best efforts in preparing this book, they make no representations or warranties with respect to the accuracy or completeness of the contents of this book and specifically disclaim any implied warranties of merchantability or fitness for a particular purpose. No warranty may be created or extended by sales representatives or written sales materials. The advice and strategies contained herein may not be suitable for your situation. You should consult with a professional when appropriate. Neither the publisher nor the author shall be liable for any loss of profit or any other commercial damages, including but not limited to special, incidental, consequential, personal, or other damages.

Contents

INTRODUCTION

Your Journey to Financial Independence Begins Now

Hey there! Welcome to your first step on a journey that could change your entire future.

Just imagine this scenario for a moment: you're out with friends, and instead of worrying about whether you have enough money, you feel totally in control.

You know exactly how much you can spend, how much you're saving, and how your money is working to make even more money for you. Sounds awesome, right?

Well, that's exactly what learning these *10 Money Skills* can do for you.

This scenario isn't just a dream - it's a realistic outcome of developing strong financial literacy. By understanding concepts like budgeting, saving, and investing, you'll gain the ability to make informed decisions about your money.

This knowledge will empower you to confidently manage your finances, whether you're deciding on a purchase or planning for your future.

Why Money Skills Matter (Especially for Teens)

Many teens think money management is boring. But in fact, it's actually a superpower that lets you control your future.

Did you know some millionaires started their first business as teenagers? You have that same potential.

Most of us don't learn about money in school. We learn about math, science, history, and even how to play the recorder, but not about something as important as managing money.

And yet, money is something you'll deal with every single day of your life. Understanding money now can help you choose a great career path later. Teens who learn money skills often become more confident and independent.

Whether it's paying for a new phone, game console or college, buying your first car, starting a business, or just hanging out with friends, knowing how to handle money will give you the freedom and confidence to make great choices.

Most schools lack financial education, which creates a gap in knowledge and can lead to poor financial decisions later in life. By being proactive and learning about money management now, you're closing this gap and setting yourself up for success.

These skills will help you navigate complex financial situations, from understanding student loans to making informed career choices based on financial considerations. Money isn't about spending. It's about creating opportunities and harnessing your dreams.

The earlier you learn how money works, the more time you have to make it work for you. Starting now, as a teenager, gives you a huge head start.

You'll learn how to save, budget, invest, and make smart money decisions that will set you up for success in the future.

This early start is crucial because of the power of compound interest. The sooner you begin saving and investing, the more time your money has to grow.

For example, if you start investing $100 a month at age 15 and continue until you're 65, you could potentially have over $1 million, assuming an average annual return of 8%.

This proves that getting a head start on your finances as a teenager is incredibly beneficial.

What You'll Learn in This Book

This book is packed with real-life tips, easy-to-understand examples, and practical exercises that you can start using right away. We'll cover:

1. **Setting Financial Goals** – Because if you don't know where you're going, how will you get there?

2. **Budgeting** – The hidden weapon for managing your money

without feeling restricted.

3. **Saving and Investing** – How to make your money grow like a superhero's sidekick.

4. **Earning Money** – From part-time jobs to creative side hustles.

5. **Avoiding Debt and Scams** – So you don't fall into the common traps that many people do.

6. **Giving Back** – Because wealth isn't about keeping money - it's also about sharing and making the world a better place.

These are all important for building a good financial base. For instance, setting financial goals helps you create a roadmap for your future, while budgeting confirms you're allocating your resources effectively to reach those goals.

Saving and investing are crucial for long-term wealth building, while learning about earning money can help you increase your income potential.

Understanding how to avoid debt and scams protects your financial well-being, and learning about giving back helps you use your wealth responsibly and meaningfully.

How to Use This Book

Each chapter will teach you a new skill, and at the end, there will be a practical exercise or activity. Take your time, and don't worry if some concepts seem new or challenging.

This is a marathon, not a sprint. The goal is to build lifelong habits that will help you create wealth and achieve financial freedom.

These exercises are designed to reinforce the concepts you've learned and help you apply them to your own life. They include activities like creating your first budget, researching different savings accounts, or brainstorming potential side hustle ideas.

By actively engaging with these exercises, you'll be more likely to keep the information and develop practical financial skills.

Ready to get started?

1. Setting Financial Goals That Matter

Picture this: You're at the mall with friends, and you spot the latest sneakers you've been eyeing for weeks. You want them, but you also have a goal to save money for a new phone.

What do you do?

This is where financial goals come in handy – they help you make smart decisions about your money.

Why Set Financial Goals?

Setting goals is like using GPS on a road trip. If you don't know where you're going, you might end up lost or just wandering around. With money, it's the same thing. Goals give you direction, help you focus, and keep you motivated.

Financial goals are essential because they provide a clear framework for your spending and saving habits. When you have a specific target in mind, it becomes easier to prioritize your expenses and make informed choices about where your money goes.

This clarity can significantly reduce impulse purchases and help you allocate your resources more effectively.

Benefits of Setting Financial Goals:

- **Gives You a Sense of Control**: You know exactly what you're working towards. This sense of control extends beyond just your finances - it can greatly impact your overall well-being and reduce stress related to money matters.
- **Helps You Make Better Decisions**: You can decide whether spending money now is worth it or if saving it for a goal makes more sense. This benefit is particularly crucial when faced with tempting purchases that might derail your long-term goals.

- **Keeps You Motivated**: When you see progress toward your goal, it feels amazing and makes you want to keep going. This motivation can be a powerful force in maintaining good financial habits over time, even when faced with challenges or setbacks.

Types of Financial Goals

Let's break it down into three types of goals:

1. **Short-Term Goals (0-6 months)**: These are things you want to achieve soon. For example, saving $100 for a concert ticket or $50 for a new video game. Short-term goals are great for building momentum and developing good financial habits quickly.

2. **Medium-Term Goals (6 months-2 years)**: These take a little longer but are still totally doable. Think about saving for a new bike or a summer camp trip. Medium-term goals help you practice delayed gratification and improve your planning skills.

3. **Long-Term Goals (2+ years)**: These require more patience and planning. It could be saving for college, a car, or even your first apartment. Long-term goals teach you the value of consistent effort and the power of compound growth over time.

How to Set SMART Financial Goals

A ***SMART*** goal isn't just smart - it's also:

- **Specific**: Know exactly what you want (e.g., "Save $300 for a new laptop"). Being specific helps you visualize your goal and makes it more tangible, increasing your commitment to achieving it.

- **Measurable**: Track your progress (e.g., "I've saved $150 so far, halfway there!"). Measurable goals allow you to see your advancement, which can be incredibly motivating and help you adjust your strategies if needed.

- **Achievable**: Make sure it's realistic. Saving $1,000 in a month might be tough, but saving $100 might be more doable. Setting achievable goals prevents discouragement and builds confidence in your ability to manage money effectively.

- **Relevant**: It should matter to you. Choose goals that fit your values and needs. Relevant goals ensure that you're working towards something that truly aligns with your personal aspirations and lifestyle.

- **Time-bound**: Set a deadline (e.g., "I want to save $300 in 4 months"). Having a timeframe creates a sense of urgency and helps you stay focused on your goal.

Example of a SMART Goal: "I want to save $200 for a pair of wireless earbuds by the end of 3 months. I'll put aside $20 from my allowance each week to reach this goal."

Creating Your First Financial Goal

Let's put this into action. Grab a notebook or open a notes app on your phone and write down your first financial goal using the SMART framework.

Practical Exercise:

1. Think of something you really want to save for.
2. Write down your goal using the SMART format.
3. Break down your goal into smaller, weekly savings targets.

Example: If your goal is to save $100 in 2 months, figure out how much you need to save each week. ($100 ÷ 8 weeks = $12.50 per week).

Breaking down your goal into smaller, manageable chunks makes it less overwhelming and easier to track. This approach also allows you to make adjustments more easily if you encounter unexpected expenses or income changes.

Staying Motivated

It's normal to feel excited when you first set a goal and then lose motivation after a while. Here's how to stay on track:

- **Visual Reminders**: Put a photo of your goal (like the sneakers you want) somewhere you'll see it every day. Visual cues can be powerful motivators, constantly reminding you of what you're working towards and why it matters to you.
- **Celebrate Small Wins**: Did you save $20 this week? Awesome! Give yourself a pat on the back and maybe treat yourself with a small, affordable reward. Acknowledging your

progress, no matter how small, reinforces positive behavior and keeps you motivated for the long haul.

- **Tell a Friend**: Share your goal with a friend or family member who can help keep you accountable. Having someone to check in with often leads to support, encouragement, and gentle reminders to stay on track.

Tip: Write your goals in a place you can see often – maybe on your phone's lock screen or a sticky note on your mirror. The more you see it, the more motivated you'll be to stick to it.

Constant visibility helps combine your financial goals into your daily life, making them a natural part of your decision-making process. By the end of this chapter, you should have at least one solid financial goal written down and a plan for how to reach it. Great job!

Now, you've got a roadmap to guide your financial decisions. Up next, we'll dive into the heart of money management.

2. Budgeting Knowhow (with a Simple Budget Template)

Alright, you've got your financial goals set. Now it's time to tackle one of the most important skills for managing your money: **budgeting.**

I know, I know – the word "budget" might sound boring or make you think of limits and restrictions.

But, a budget isn't about saying "no" to things you want. It's actually about giving you the freedom to say "yes" to what matters most.

Think of a budget as your personal money plan, a guide that helps you decide how to spend, save, and grow your money. When you have a budget, you're in control, and that's a pretty awesome feeling.

What Is a Budget and Why Do You Need One?

A budget is simply a plan that shows:

- How much money you have coming in (income)
- How much money is going out (expenses)

Creating a budget helps you:

- **See where your money is going:** No more wondering where all your cash disappeared to!
- **Make sure you don't overspend:** It keeps you from spending more money than you actually have.
- **Reach your financial goals faster:** By managing your money wisely, you can save for things you really care about.

Imagine this... You get $100 for your birthday. Without a budget, you might spend it all on random things and not even remember what you bought.

With a budget, you can decide to put $50 towards your savings goal, $30 for something fun, and $20 for snacks or treats.

It's all about balance!

The 50/30/20 Rule: A Simple Way to Budget

A popular and easy way to budget is the 50/30/20 rule. Here's how it works:

- **50% for Needs:** These are things you absolutely have to pay for, like school supplies, bus fare, or lunch money.
- **30% for Wants:** These are things you like to spend money on, like snacks, movies, or new clothes.
- **20% for Savings:** This is the money you put aside for your goals, emergencies, or investments.

Example: Let's say you earn $200 a month from a part-time job. Using the 50/30/20 rule, you'd budget:

- $100 for needs
- $60 for wants
- $40 for savings

This way, you're covering what's necessary, enjoying life, and still saving for the future.

Creating Your First Budget

Let's break this down step by step. Grab a pen and paper, open a notes app, or use the budget template below.

Step 1: List Your Income

Write down all the money you expect to receive each month. This could include:

- Allowance
- Money from part-time jobs or side hustles
- Gifts or birthday money

Example:

- Part-time job: $150
- Allowance: $50
- Total Income: $200

Step 2: List Your Expenses

Think about everything you spend money on. Group your expenses into two categories:

- Needs: School supplies, transportation, phone bill, etc.
- Wants: Eating out, new clothes, entertainment, etc.

Example:

- Needs: $80 (lunch money, bus fare, phone bill)
- Wants: $60 (snacks, movie tickets)
- Savings: $60

Step 3: Balance Your Budget

Add up your income and your expenses. If your expenses are more than your income, you need to make some adjustments.

Either cut back on your wants or find ways to increase your income.

Example:

- Total Income: $200
- Total Expenses: $200 (This is a balanced budget!)

Simple Budget Template

Here's a simple budget template you can use. Feel free to customize it based on your needs.

SIMPLE BUDGET TEMPLATE

Month: **Year:**

Category	Planned Amount	Actual Amount
Income		
Part-time job	$ 150	
Allowance	$ 50	
Other	$ -	
Total Income	$ 200	
Expenses		
Needs		
Lunch Money	$ 30	
Bus Fare	$ 20	
Phone Bill	$ 30	
Other	$ -	
Other	$ -	
Total Needs	$ 80	
Wants		
Snacks	$ 20	
Entertainment	$ 40	
Other	$ -	
Other	$ -	
Total Wants	$ 60	
Savings	$ 60	
Total Expenses	$ 200	

Fill in your own numbers and see how they add up. If your expenses are more than your income, look for areas where you can cut back.

Common Budgeting Mistakes (and How to Avoid Them)

1. **Not Tracking Your Spending**: It's easy to lose track of where your money goes if you don't write it down. Use a budgeting app or keep a note on your phone to track every purchase.
2. **Forgetting to Budget for Fun**: A budget doesn't mean you can't have fun. Make sure to include some spending money for things you enjoy - just don't go overboard.
3. **Not Saving at All**: Even if it's just a small amount, try to save something every month.

The habit of saving is more important than the amount at first.

Practical Exercise: Create Your Own Budget

1. Write down your total income for the month.
2. List out your needs and wants.
3. Use the 50/30/20 rule to allocate your money.
4. Track your spending throughout the month and see how it matches your budget.

Tip: Review your budget at the end of the month. Did you spend more or less than you planned?

Adjust your budget for the next month based on what you learned.

Budgeting Tools for Teens

There are lots of apps and tools that can make budgeting easier. Here are a few to check out:

- Mint: Helps you track your income, expenses, and savings goals.
- YNAB (You Need A Budget): Great for helping you plan where every dollar goes.
- Google Sheets or Excel: If you like spreadsheets, these are easy to customize.

Bonus Tip: Set up an automatic transfer to your savings account each month. This way, you save without even thinking about it!

The Benefits of Sticking to a Budget

When you follow a budget, you'll notice some amazing things happening:

- You'll feel more in control of your money.
- You'll be able to save faster and reach your goals sooner.
- You'll stress less about money because you know exactly where it's going.

Fabulous! You've just created your first budget. This skill alone can help you achieve big things in life, from saving for a car to planning for college.

In the next chapter, we'll dive into the art of saving and show you how to build your very first $1,000.

3. The Importance of Saving: How to Build Your First $1,000

Great job on learning how to budget! Now that you have a plan for your money, it's time to talk about one of the most important money skills: **Saving**.

Saving might sound simple, but it's the key to building wealth and reaching your goals.

Whether you want to buy a new phone, save for a car, or have an emergency fund, saving money is the first step.

Why Saving Is Important

Saving money isn't about putting cash aside - this involves building a habit that can change your life. Here's why saving is so powerful:

1. **It Gives You Freedom**: Having savings means you don't have to rely on others or go into debt when something unexpected happens. This financial independence allows you to make choices based on what's best for you, rather than being forced into decisions because of lack of funds.

2. **It Helps You Reach Your Goals**: Whether it's a concert ticket, a new gadget, or a big trip, saving helps you get what you want without stress. By setting aside money regularly, you can work towards both short-term wants and long-term aspirations without feeling overwhelmed.

3. **It Builds Good Habits**: When you start saving as a teen, you develop habits that will help you for the rest of your life. The discipline of saving regularly teaches you patience, delayed gratification, and financial responsibility – skills that are valuable in many areas of life beyond just money management.

Think about this: If you save just $10 a week, that's over $500 in a year! Small amounts add up over time.

This principle of consistent, small actions leading to significant results applies to saving money but to many other aspects of personal growth and achievement.

The 3 Types of Savings Everyone Needs

To make saving easier, divide your savings into three main categories:

1. **Emergency Fund**: This is money set aside for unexpected expenses, like a surprise bill or a broken phone. Aim to save at least $500 for emergencies. An emergency fund acts as a financial buffer, protecting you from having to borrow money or use credit cards when unforeseen circumstances arise.

2. **Short-Term Savings**: These are for things you want in the near future, like a new pair of sneakers or a trip with friends. Short-term savings help you avoid impulse purchases and allow you to plan for expenses you know are coming up in the next few months to a year.

3. **Long-Term Savings**: This is for bigger goals that take longer to reach, like saving for college or a car. Long-term savings require more patience but can have a significant impact on your future financial stability and opportunities.

How to Start Saving (Even If You Don't Make Much Money)

You might be thinking, "But I don't have a lot of money to save!" That's okay. The goal is to start small and build the habit.

Here are some tips:

- **Pay Yourself First**: This means setting aside money for savings before you spend on anything else. Even if it's just $5 or $10, put it into your savings account first.

This strategy confirms that saving becomes a priority rather than an afterthought.

- **Automate Your Savings**: If you have a bank account, set up an automatic transfer to your savings every time you get paid. This way, you don't even have to think about it.

Automation removes the temptation to spend the money elsewhere and makes saving a consistent, efficient habit.

- **Save Your Change**: Use a jar to collect spare change or small bills. It might not seem like much, but it adds up faster than you think.

This method can be particularly effective because it turns saving into a tangible, visual activity.

- **Cut Back on Small Expenses**: Look at your budget and see if there are small expenses you can reduce, like fewer snacks from the vending machine or fewer trips to the coffee shop. These small changes can have a big impact over time without significantly affecting your daily life.

Example: If you save $1.50 every day by skipping a soda or snack, that's $45 in a month and $540 in a year! This example illustrates how small, consistent savings can accumulate into significant amounts over time.

The $1,000 Savings Challenge

Let's make saving fun with a challenge! Your goal is to save your first $1,000. Here's a simple plan to help you get there:

1. **Set a Timeline**: Decide when you want to reach your $1,000 goal. Let's say you want to do it in 6 months. Setting a specific timeframe helps create urgency and motivation.

2. **Break It Down**: Divide your goal by the number of weeks in your timeline. If you have 6 months (about 26 weeks), you need to save around $38.50 per week. Breaking down a large goal into smaller, manageable chunks makes it feel more achievable and helps you track your progress more easily.

3. **Track Your Progress**: Use a savings tracker or make a chart to see your progress. Celebrate each milestone, like when you reach $100, $500, and finally $1,000. Tracking and celebrating milestones provides motivation and a sense of accomplishment along the way.

Tip: Create a visual tracker, like a savings thermometer, and color it in as you get closer to your goal. It's a great way to stay motivated!

Visual representations of your progress can be powerful motivators, making your goal feel more tangible and achievable.

Opening a Savings Account

If you don't already have a savings account, now is a great time to open one. Here's what you need to know:

- **Choose the Right Bank**: Look for a bank or credit union with no monthly fees and a good interest rate for savings accounts. Research different options and compare their features to find the best fit for your needs.

- **Ask About Teen Accounts**: Many banks offer special accounts for teens with lower fees and tools to help you learn about saving. These accounts often come with educational resources and may have features designed specifically for younger savers.
- **Start with a Deposit**: Even if you only have $20 to start, that's okay. The important thing is to get started and keep adding to it.

Every savings journey begins with that first deposit, no matter how small.

The Magic of Compound Interest (the next chapter goes into this in more detail)

Have you heard of compound interest? It's like giving your money superpowers.

Here's how it works: when you put money in a savings account, the bank pays you interest, which is like a reward for saving.

Then, you start earning interest on both your original money and the interest you've already earned. This makes your savings grow faster over time.

Example: Let's say you save $1,000 in a savings account that pays 5% interest per year. After one year, you'll have $1,050.

But next year, you earn interest on $1,050, not just $1,000.

This means your money grows even faster each year. Compound interest is a powerful force in building wealth over time, especially when you start saving early.

Practical Exercise: Calculate Your Savings Growth

1. Choose an amount you want to save (e.g., $500).
2. Use an online compound interest calculator (just search "compound interest calculator") to see how your savings can grow over 5, 10, or even 20 years.
3. Play around with different interest rates and monthly contributions to see the impact.

This exercise helps you visualize the long-term benefits of saving and the power of compound interest. It can be a powerful motivator to see how your money can grow over time.

Saving Tips from Real Teens

Here are some creative ways other teens are saving money:

- **Sell Unwanted Items**: Have old clothes, books, or gadgets you don't use? Sell them online or at a garage sale and put the money into savings.

This helps you declutter and turns unused items into cash for your savings goals.

- **Start a Savings Challenge with Friends**: Compete with friends to see who can save the most money in a month. It's a fun way to stay motivated.

Social support and friendly competition can make saving more enjoyable and help you stay accountable.

- **Use Cash Instead of Cards**: It's harder to spend money when you have to hand over actual cash. Try using cash for a week and see if it helps you save more.

This method can make you more aware of your spending habits and help you make more conscious decisions about purchases.

Practical Exercise: Create a Savings Plan

Let's make a plan to start saving today!

1. Write down your savings goal (e.g., "I want to save $200 for a new pair of headphones").

2. Decide how much you can save each week or month.

3. Track your progress.

Use a savings jar, a notebook, or a digital tracker to see how close you are to your goal.

Example: To save $200 in 3 months, that's about $67 per month or $16.75 per week. Can you find a way to cut back on small expenses to make this happen?

This exercise helps you practice setting specific, measurable goals and breaking them down into actionable steps.

The Reward of Saving

When you finally reach your savings goal, it's going to feel amazing! Not only will you have the money you need for what you want, but you'll also have the confidence of knowing you set a goal and achieved it.

Plus, you'll have built a habit that will help you throughout your life.

Saving is a skill that grows stronger the more you use it. So, start small, be consistent, and watch your savings grow.

Up next, we'll talk about how to make your money work even harder for you with the power of investing.

Ready to learn how to grow your wealth even faster?

4. Understanding the Magic of Compound Interest

You've learned how to save money and create a plan for building your first $1,000. Now, it's time to unlock one of the most powerful secrets of wealth creation: **Compound interest**.

Think of compound interest as the superhero of the financial world – it's like having your own money machine that works for you, even when you're asleep.

What Is Compound Interest?

Compound interest is the interest you earn on the money you save and on the interest you've already earned. In other words, it's interest on interest.

This might sound confusing, but don't worry – we'll break it down with some easy examples.

Imagine This: You plant a small apple tree. At first, it grows a few apples, which you can eat.

But instead of eating all of them, you plant some of the seeds.

Over time, those seeds grow into new trees, which produce even more apples. That's how compound interest works – it keeps growing on itself!

Simple Interest vs. Compound Interest

Before we look further, let's compare simple interest and compound interest:

- **Simple Interest:** You earn interest only on the original amount you saved (the principal). It's straightforward but doesn't grow very fast.

- **Compound Interest:** You earn interest on the original amount and on the interest that has already been added. This makes your money grow much faster over time.

Example:

- If you save $100 at a 5% interest rate for 5 years:
- With simple interest, you'd earn $5 each year, so after 5 years, you'd have $125.
- With compound interest, the interest grows each year, so after 5 years, you'd have about $128. It might not seem like a big difference at first, but the gap gets bigger the longer you leave your money to grow.

The Rule of 72: How to Double Your Money

The Rule of 72 is a quick way to estimate how long it will take for your money to double with compound interest. All you have to do is divide 72 by the interest rate.

Example: If you have an interest rate of 6%, divide 72 by 6. It will take about 12 years for your money to double.

This might sound like a long time, but remember, you're doing this without lifting a finger – your money is working for you!

Why Starting Early Matters

The biggest advantage you have as a teenager is time. The earlier you start saving and investing, the more time your money has to grow with compound interest.

Example: Let's say two friends, Alex and Taylor, decide to start saving:

- Alex starts saving $50 a month at age 15 and stops at age 25.

Over those 10 years, Alex saves $6,000.

- Taylor waits until age 25 to start saving but saves $50 a month until age 35 (10 years as well). Taylor also saves $6,000.
- By age 40, who has more money? Surprisingly, Alex has more money because the money had more time to grow with compound interest, even though they both saved the same amount.

This is why starting early is so important – your money gets more time to compound!

How to Make Compound Interest Work for You

Here are a few ways you can start using compound interest to grow your savings:

1. **Open a High-Interest Savings Account:** Look for a savings account with a good interest rate (even 2% or 3% can make a big difference over time). When choosing a savings account, consider factors such as least balance requirements, fees, and accessibility. Online banks often offer higher interest rates than traditional brick-and-mortar banks.
2. **Invest in Stocks or Mutual Funds:** These can offer higher returns than a savings account, but they also come with more risk. We'll talk more about investing in the next chapter. It's important to understand that while stocks and mutual funds can potentially yield higher returns, they also carry the risk of losing value. Always research and consider your risk

tolerance before investing.

3. **Reinvest Your Interest:** Instead of taking out the interest you earn, leave it in your account so it can compound and grow even more. This strategy allows your money to grow exponentially over time, as you're earning interest on both your principal and the accumulated interest.

Practical Exercise: See Compound Interest in Action

Grab your phone or computer and search for a compound interest calculator online. Here's what to do:

1. Enter an initial savings amount (like $500).
2. Choose an interest rate (try 5%).
3. Set a time period (like 10 years).
4. Click "calculate" and see how much your savings grow over time.

Try changing the interest rate or the time period to see how it affects the total amount. You'll see that even small changes can make a big difference when compound interest is involved.

Tip: The longer you leave your money to grow, the bigger the impact of compound interest. This is why it's often called "the eighth wonder of the world."

The Power of Consistency

The key to making compound interest work for you is consistency. Even if you can only save a small amount each month, it will grow significantly over time.

Here's why:

- **Consistency Builds Habits:** Saving regularly becomes part of your routine, making it easier to stay on track. By making saving a habit, you're more likely to stick with it long-term, even when faced with financial challenges or temptations.

- **You Don't Need a Lot of Money:** Even small amounts can grow into big sums thanks to compound interest. Don't be discouraged if you can only save a little at first.

The important thing is to start and maintain the habit of saving regularly.

- **It Reduces Risk:** By saving and investing regularly, you spread out your risk and take advantage of the power of time. This strategy, known as dollar-cost averaging, can help mitigate the impact of market fluctuations on your investments over the long term.

Example: If you save just $20 a month from age 15 to age 25 (10 years), you'll have invested $2,400. With compound interest at a 5% rate, your savings could grow to over $3,000.

That's $600 more just from interest – and you didn't have to do anything extra!

Don't Be Afraid to Start Small

You might be thinking, "I don't have a lot of money to invest or save." That's okay! The important thing is to start, even if it's with small amounts.

Over time, those small amounts will grow, and you'll be impressed at the results.

Practical Exercise: Start Your Own Savings Account

If you haven't already, open a savings account and make your first deposit. Even if it's just $10 or $20, get into the habit of putting money into your account regularly.

Set a goal to add something every week, even if it's just a few dollars.

When opening a savings account, consider factors such as least balance requirements, fees, and accessibility. Look for accounts specifically designed for young savers, as they often have more favorable terms.

Bonus Tip: Set up an automatic transfer from your checking account to your savings account. This way, you'll be saving without even thinking about it.

Automating your savings helps confirm that you consistently set aside money, reducing the temptation to spend it elsewhere.

Compound Interest: The Wealth Multiplier

Let's recap why compound interest is such a game-changer:

- It helps your money grow faster than simple interest.

- It rewards you for starting early and being consistent.
- It's like a snowball rolling down a hill – the longer it rolls, the bigger it gets.

In the next chapter, we're going to build on what you've learned here and dive into the exciting world of investing. You'll learn how to make your money work even harder for you by buying stocks, bonds, and other investments.

Ready to take your financial knowledge to the next level?

5. Investing 101: Making Your Money Work for You

Now that you have your savings started, and you've learned how to harness the power of compound interest, it's time to take things up a notch and learn about investing.

Investing is like planting a seed – you put in a little bit of money, give it time to grow, and hopefully, it turns into something much bigger.

The earlier you start, the bigger your investment can grow over time.

What Is Investing?

Investing means using your money to buy things that you believe will grow in value over time. Instead of just saving your money in a bank account, you're putting it into something that can earn you even more money.

This could be stocks, bonds, real estate, cryptocurrency or even starting your own business.

Picture This: If you buy a share of a company like Apple or Nike, you own a tiny piece of that company. If the company does well, your share becomes more valuable, and you can sell it for a profit.

This means that as the company grows, introduces new products, or increases it's profits, the value of your share is likely to increase as well.

However, be aware that the opposite can also happen – if the company performs poorly, your share value could decrease.

Why Should You Start Investing as a Teen?

The biggest advantage you have as a teenager is time. Here's why starting to invest early is a huge benefit:

1. **More Time for Growth**: The longer you leave your investments, the more time they have to grow. Remember compound interest? It works even better with investments. This is because when you reinvest your earnings (like dividends from stocks), you're essentially earning returns on

your returns, which can significantly accelerate your wealth accumulation over time.

2. **Learn Early, Succeed Later**: The earlier you start, the more time you have to learn from your mistakes and improve your investing skills. This means you can make smaller, less impactful mistakes when you're young and have less money at stake, as opposed to making costly errors later in life when you have more to lose.

3. **Build Wealth Over Time**: Investing is one of the best ways to grow your money faster than saving alone. It's how many people build long-term wealth. By investing, you're putting your money to work, potentially earning returns that outpace inflation and grow your purchasing power over time.

Fun Fact: If you start investing $50 a month at age 15 and earn an average return of 8% per year, you could have over $150,000 by the time you're 50. If you wait until you're 25 to start, you'd only have about $78,000.

That's what's so important about starting early!

This example illustrates the significant impact of compound interest over time, showing how even a small amount invested regularly can grow substantially when given enough time.

Types of Investments

There are many different ways to invest your money, but let's focus on a few of the most common ones that are great for beginners.

1. Stocks

A stock is a share in a company. When you buy a stock, you become a part-owner of that company. Stocks can go up and down in value depending on how well the company is doing.

- Pros: High potential returns if the company does well.
- Cons: Higher risk - stocks can lose value, especially in the short term.

Example: If you bought a share of Tesla for $100 and it goes up to $150, you've made a $50 profit. But if the stock drops to $80, you've lost $20 (on paper, until you sell it). If for example if you bought 1 stock in Apple in January 2020 for around $76 it's value as at the end of November 2024 was around $230. During this time Apple paid investors dividends (a reward for holding you share) which you could choose to reinvest back into the company (by buying more stocks), recieve the cash or buy other stocks.

It's important to understand that stock prices can be volatile, meaning they can change rapidly based on various factors such as company performance, market conditions, or even global events.

This is why it's crucial to consider your risk tolerance and investment timeline when investing in stocks.

2. Bonds

Bonds are like loans that you give to a company or government. In return, they promise to pay you back with interest. Bonds are usually safer than stocks but have lower returns.

- Pros: Lower risk, steady income.
- Cons: Lower potential returns compared to stocks.

Example: If you buy a $100 bond with a 5% interest rate, you'll earn $5 per year in interest until the bond matures (when the company pays you back your $100). Bonds are generally considered less risky than stocks because they provide a fixed income stream and return of principal at maturity.

However, be aware that bonds are not risk-free – factors such as interest rate changes and the issuer's creditworthiness can affect their value.

3. Mutual Funds and ETFs

A mutual fund or an ETF (Exchange-Traded Fund) is a collection of stocks and bonds bundled together. Instead of buying individual stocks, you buy a small piece of many investments at once. This helps you spread out your risk (diversification) because you're not relying on just one company to do well.

- Pros: Diversification, professional management.
- Cons: Fees, and sometimes less control over individual investments.

Example: If you invest in a mutual fund that holds 100 different stocks, your money is spread out across all of them. Even if one stock loses value, others might go up, balancing out the risk.

This diversification can help protect your investment from the poor performance of any single company.

However, it's important to understand that while diversification can reduce risk, it doesn't eliminate it entirely – market-wide downturns can still affect diversified portfolios.

4. Real Estate

Real estate investing involves buying property (like a house or apartment) and earning money through rent or by selling it for more than you paid. This type of investment usually requires more money upfront and is less common for teenagers but can be a great long-term goal.

- Pros: Steady income, property value can increase over time.
- Cons: High initial cost, requires maintenance.

Real estate investing can provide both ongoing income (through rent) and potential long-term appreciation. However, it's important to consider factors such as property taxes, maintenance costs, and the potential for periods without tenants when calculating the potential returns from real estate investments.

5. Cryptocurrency

Cryptocurrency is a type of money that only exists online (virtual currency). It's digital, and instead of being controlled by a bank or government, it's run by a system called blockchain, which keeps everything secure and transparent.

Pros:

- **You could make a lot of money:** Some cryptocurrencies, like Bitcoin, have gone way up in value over time.
- **Secure and private:** Your transactions are safe and can't easily be hacked or changed.

Cons:

- **Prices can go up and down really fast:** You could make a lot of money, but you could lose it just as quickly.

- **Not everyone uses it yet:** You can't spend cryptocurrency in most stores or places.

Example:

Let's say you buy 1 Bitcoin for $30,000. If its price goes up to $40,000, you've made $10,000. But if it drops to $20,000, you've lost $10,000 (unless you hold onto it, hoping the price goes back up).

People who bought just 1 Bitcoin back in January 2020 would have paid around $7,000 and as at the end of November 2024 the value was about $96,000. Wow! However during that almost 5 year period the value went from about $7,000 to $61,000 (January 2021) to $46,000 (January 2022) to $16,000 (January 2023) to $42,000 (January 2024).

So you can see how volatile this can be and you really need nerves of steel! Cryptocurrency can be exciting because it can grow quickly, but it's also risky because prices change so much. If you're interested, it's a good idea to start small and learn as much as you can!

How to Get Started with Investing as a Teen

As a teenager, you might not be able to open a brokerage account on your own just yet, but there are still ways to start investing:

1. **Open a Custodial Account**: Ask a parent or guardian to help you open a custodial brokerage account. This allows you to start investing with their help until you turn 18 (or 21 in some places). A custodial account is legally owned by the minor, but managed by an adult until the minor reaches the age of majority.

1. **Use Investing Apps for Teens**: There are apps designed specifically for young investors that make it easy to start small with as little as $5. These apps often provide educational resources and simplified interfaces to help beginners learn about investing.

2. **Invest in Index Funds or ETFs**: These are great for beginners because they offer diversification and usually have lower fees. Index funds and ETFs track a specific market index, providing broad market exposure with a single investment.

Tip: Start with small amounts and invest regularly, even if it's just $10 a month. Consistency is key!

Regular investing, also known as dollar-cost averaging, can help smooth out the impact of market volatility over time.

Understanding Risk and Reward

All investments come with some level of risk. Generally, the higher the potential reward, the higher the risk.

Here's what you need to know:

- **Low-Risk Investments**: Bonds, savings accounts. These are safer but grow more slowly. While they offer more stability, their returns may not keep pace with inflation over the long term.

- **Medium-Risk Investments**: Index funds, ETFs. They offer good growth potential with moderate risk. These investments provide diversification across many companies or sectors, which can help balance risk and reward.

- **High-Risk Investments**: Individual stocks, cryptocurrency. These can offer big rewards and come with a higher chance of losing money. It's important to thoroughly research and understand these investments before committing funds.

Rule of Thumb: Don't invest money you can't afford to lose, and never put all your money into one type of investment. This helps protect you from significant losses and ensures you maintain financial stability while investing.

The Importance of Diversification

Diversification is a fancy word for not putting all your eggs in one basket. By spreading your money across different types of investments, you reduce the risk of losing it all if one investment doesn't do well.

Example: If you have $1000 to invest, don't put all of it into a single stock. Instead, you could put $500 into an ETF, $100 into bonds, and $250 into individual stocks and $150 into cryptocurrency.

This way, your risk is spread out.

Diversification doesn't just mean investing in different stocks – it also involves spreading investments across different asset classes (like stocks, bonds, real estate and cryptocurrencies) and different sectors of the economy.

Practical Exercise: Create a Mock Investment Portfolio

Let's practice what you've learned:

1. Choose four different types of investments you'd like to in-

clude in your portfolio (e.g., one stock, one ETF, and one crypto).

2. Use an investing app's "watchlist" feature to track their performance for a month.

3. Write down why you chose each investment and what you hope to gain from it.

Example Portfolio:

- Stock: Apple ($50)
- ETF: S&P 500 Index Fund ($30)
- Bond: U.S. Treasury Bond ($20)

Track the changes and see how your portfolio performs over time. This exercise can help you understand how different investments behave and how external factors can affect their performance.

Investing Tips for Teens

1. **Start Small**: Even $5 or $10 can grow into a lot over time thanks to compound interest. Starting small allows you to learn and gain confidence without risking large amounts of money.

2. **Do Your Research**: Learn about the companies you're investing in and why you think they'll do well. This includes understanding their business model, competitive advantages, and potential risks.

1. **Think Long-Term**: Investing is a marathon, not a sprint. Don't worry about daily ups and downs. Focus on the long-term potential of your investments and avoid making decisions based on short-term market fluctuations.

2. **Ask Questions**: If you're unsure about something, ask a trusted adult or do some research online.

Never invest in something you don't understand.

Final Thoughts on Investing

Investing can seem scary at first, but it's one of the best ways to build wealth over time. The most important thing is to start, even if you don't have a lot of money.

By learning and investing consistently, you're setting yourself up for financial success in the future.

In the next chapter, we're going to dive into credit and debt. We'll talk about how to build good credit and avoid the traps of debt that can hold you back.

Ready to keep learning?

6. Credit and Debt: Building Good Credit and Avoiding the problems

We've covered a lot of ground so far – setting goals, budgeting, saving, and even investing. **You're well on your way** to mastering money skills that will set you up for success.

Now it's time to dive into a topic that can be a little tricky but is super important: **Credit and debt.**

Understanding how these work is essential because they can either help you build wealth or create financial problems if you're not careful.

What Is Credit?

Credit is the ability to borrow money or access goods and services with the promise to pay it back later. When someone lends you money or allows you to buy something without paying upfront, they're giving you credit.

But there's a catch: you need to pay back what you borrow, often with extra money called interest. This interest is essentially the cost of borrowing money, and it's how lenders make a profit from extending credit.

Imagine This: You borrow $20 from a friend to buy a concert ticket, promising to pay them back next week. Your friend is giving you credit. If you take too long to pay them back or forget entirely, they might not trust you again.

This simple scenario illustrates the basic principle of credit: trust and the expectation of repayment.

How Does Credit Work?

When you use credit, like a credit card or a loan, the lender expects you to pay back the amount borrowed. If you pay it back on time, you build good credit, which shows lenders you're responsible.

If you don't pay it back or make late payments, it can hurt your credit score and make it harder to borrow money in the future. It's important to understand that credit isn't free money. When you use credit, you're essentially borrowing from your future self.

The key is to use credit strategically and responsibly, always keeping in mind that you'll need to repay what you borrow, often with interest.

What Is a Credit Score?

A credit score is a number that tells lenders how trustworthy you are when it comes to borrowing money. It's like a report card for your financial responsibility, and it usually ranges from 300 to 850. The higher your score, the better.

Your credit score is calculated based on several factors, including your payment history, the amount of debt you have, the length of your credit history, and the types of credit you use.

- **Good Credit Score: 700 and above** – You're seen as a low-risk borrower and can get better interest rates. This means you'll pay less over time when borrowing money.

- **Fair Credit Score: 650-699** – You might get approved for loans but with higher interest rates. This means borrowing money will cost you more compared to someone with a good credit score.

- **Poor Credit Score: Below 650** – It can be tough to get approved for loans or credit cards. If you are approved, you'll likely face high interest rates, making borrowing very expensive.

How to Build Good Credit (Starting as a Teen)

Even if you're just starting out, there are things you can do now to build good credit:

1. **Open a Savings or Checking Account:** This is a simple way to show that you can manage money responsibly. While these accounts don't directly impact your credit score, they establish a relationship with a financial institution and demonstrate your ability to handle money.

2. **Become an Authorized User:** Ask a parent if you can be added as an authorized user on their credit card. You get the benefits of their good credit without having to apply for your own card yet. This can be a great way to start building credit history, but make sure the primary cardholder has a good credit history themselves.

3. **Pay Your Bills on Time:** Even if it's just your phone bill or a streaming subscription, paying on time shows lenders that you're reliable. Set up automatic payments or reminders to ensure you never miss a due date.

4. **Start with a Secured Credit Card:** When you turn 18, consider getting a secured credit card, which requires a deposit. This helps you build credit without much risk. The deposit acts as collateral, reducing the risk for the lender and making it easier for you to get approved.

Tip: Always pay your credit card balance in full every month. This way, you avoid interest charges and build good credit.

Paying in full shows that you can manage credit responsibly and don't rely on borrowing to make ends meet.

Understanding Debt: The Good, The Bad, and The Ugly

Debt is money you owe to someone else. Not all debt is bad, but it can become a problem if you take on too much or can't pay it back.

Here's what you need to know:

Good Debt vs. Bad Debt

- **Good Debt:** This is debt that can help you build wealth over time. Examples include student loans (which can lead to a higher-paying job) or a mortgage (which helps you buy a house).

Good debt typically has lower interest rates and is invested in something that has the potential to increase in value or generate income.

- **Bad Debt:** This is debt that doesn't add value and usually comes with high interest rates, like credit card debt or payday loans. It can quickly spiral out of control if you're not careful.

Bad debt is often used to purchase items that depreciate in value or for consumption rather than investment.

Example: Using a student loan to pay for college can be good debt if it leads to a better job. But using a credit card to buy expensive clothes you can't afford is usually bad debt.

The education can increase your earning potential, while the clothes will lose value and won't contribute to your financial growth.

The Dangers of High-Interest Debt

Credit cards can be helpful tools if you use them wisely, but they can also lead to high-interest debt. Here's why:

- **High Interest Rates:** Credit cards often have interest rates of 15% to 25%. If you don't pay off your balance in full, you'll end up paying much more for your purchases.

This compound interest can cause your debt to grow rapidly if not managed properly.

- **The Minimum Payment Trap:** Credit card companies let you make a small least payment each month, but this keeps you in debt longer and costs you more in interest. While it might seem easier to make smaller payments, this approach can lead to years of debt and significantly more money paid in interest.

Example: If you owe $1,000 on a credit card with a 20% interest rate and only make the least payment each month, it could take you years to pay it off and cost you hundreds of dollars in interest. For instance, if your least payment is 2% of the balance or $20 (whichever is greater), it would take you over 9 years to pay off the debt, and you'd end up paying an extra $1,581 in interest.

How to Avoid problems of Debt

1. **Only Borrow What You Can Pay Back:** If you can't afford to pay for something in cash, think twice before charging it

to a credit card. Ask yourself if the purchase is a necessity or a want, and consider saving up for it instead.

2. **Pay Your Balance in Full:** Always aim to pay off your credit card balance every month. This way, you avoid interest charges and demonstrate responsible credit use. If you can't pay in full, pay as much as you can above the least payment.

3. **Avoid Payday Loans:** These are short-term loans with extremely high interest rates. They might seem like a quick fix, but they can trap you in a cycle of debt. The high interest rates and short repayment terms make these loans very difficult to pay off, often leading to a cycle of borrowing to repay previous loans.

Practical Exercise: Plan for Responsible Credit Use

If you were given a credit card tomorrow, how would you use it? Write down three rules you'd follow to make sure you use it responsibly.

Example Rules:

1. I will only use my credit card for emergencies or planned purchases.

2. I will pay off the entire balance every month.

3. I will never spend more than 30% of my credit limit.

Credit Myths (Busted!)

There are a lot of myths about credit that can be confusing. Let's clear up a few common ones:

- **Myth 1:** You need to carry a balance to build credit.
- **Truth:** Paying off your balance in full each month is the best way to build good credit. Carrying a balance only results in unnecessary interest charges and doesn't improve your credit score.
- **Myth 2:** Checking your credit score hurts it.
- **Truth:** Checking your own score is called a "soft inquiry" and doesn't affect your score. You can check your own credit as often as you like without any negative impact.

It's actually a good habit to monitor your credit regularly.

- **Myth 3:** Closing a credit card helps your credit score.
- **Truth:** Closing a card can actually lower your score because it reduces your available credit. This can increase your credit utilization ratio, which is the amount of credit you're using compared to your total available credit.

A lower credit utilization ratio is better for your credit score.

Building Good Credit Takes Time

Building a strong credit history doesn't happen overnight, but the habits you start forming now will make a big difference later. Good credit can help you get better interest rates on loans, rent an apartment, or even land a job (some employers check credit scores!).

Consistency and patience are key – focus on making all your payments on time and managing your credit responsibly over the long term.

Tip: Set a calendar reminder to check your credit score every few months. There are free apps and websites that let you monitor your score without affecting it.

Regular monitoring can help you catch any errors or potential fraud early.

Practical Exercise: Create a Credit Plan

Think about your future goals. Do you want to buy a car? Rent an apartment?

Your credit score will play a big role in these decisions. Write down three things you can start doing now to build good credit.

Example Plan:

1. Open a savings account and deposit money regularly.
2. Become an authorized user on a parent's credit card.
3. Pay all my bills on time every month.

Final Thoughts on Credit and Debt

Credit can be a powerful tool if you use it wisely, but it can also be dangerous if you're not careful. The key is to borrow responsibly, pay back what you owe, and avoid high-interest debt whenever possible.

With good credit habits, you'll be setting yourself up for a bright financial future. Credit is a tool to help you achieve your financial goals, not a way to live beyond your means.

In the next chapter, we'll dive into avoiding financial pitfalls, problems, issues, problems, issues – the common money mistakes many teens make and how you can avoid them. Ready to keep learning?

7. Avoiding Financial Pitfalls, Problems, Issues: Mistakes Most Teens Make (and How to Avoid Them)

Great! You should be feeling pretty excited by now! But here's a secret: **even the smartest people make financial mistakes**.

It's easy to get caught up in bad habits, especially when you're just starting out.

However, you can avoid many of these common pitfalls, problems, issues, problems, issues by knowing what to look out for.

Why Teens Often Make Money Mistakes

You guys are new to managing money, and that's okay! It's normal to make mistakes as you learn, but some money problems can have long-term effects if you're not careful.

Here's why it happens:

- **Peer Pressure**: Friends are getting the latest gadgets, clothes, or shoes, and you feel like you need to keep up. This pressure can lead to overspending on items you don't really need or can't afford, just to fit in or maintain a certain image among your peers.

- **Impulse Buying**: You see something cool and buy it without thinking twice, only to regret it later. Impulse buying often occurs when emotions override logical decision-making, leading to purchases that may not align with your financial goals or needs.

- **Lack of Knowledge**: Schools don't usually teach personal finance, so many teens aren't sure how to handle their money wisely. This gap in education can lead to misunderstandings about budgeting, saving, investing, and managing credit, which can have long-lasting financial consequences.

The key is to learn from these mistakes before they happen. Let's go through some of the most common financial pitfalls, problems, issues, problems, issues and how you can avoid them.

Pitfall 1: Impulse Buying

Impulse buying is when you make a purchase without planning or thinking it through. It often happens when you're shopping online or at the mall and see something you suddenly feel like you "have to have." The problem?

These purchases can add up fast and leave you with empty pockets.

Example: You go to the mall with $50 in your pocket, planning to save it. But then you see a cool T-shirt that costs $40.

You buy it on the spot, and now you only have $10 left – no money for savings or anything else you might need.

How to Avoid Impulse Buying

- **Wait 24 Hours**: If you see something you want, wait a day before buying it. If you still want it after 24 hours, it might be worth it.

This cooling-off period allows you to evaluate whether the purchase aligns with your needs and financial goals.

- **Make a Shopping List**: Write down what you need before you go shopping and stick to it. This helps you focus on your actual needs and avoid being swayed by attractive displays or sales pitches.

- **Set a Spending Limit**: Decide how much you're willing to spend on "wants" each month and don't go over that amount. This creates a boundary for discretionary spending while ensuring you have money for necessities and savings.

Tip: Use the "30-Day Rule" for bigger purchases. If you want something expensive, wait 30 days before buying it.

Often, you'll find you don't want it as much after the wait.

This extended waiting period can help you distinguish between genuine needs and fleeting wants.

Pitfall 2: Falling for Scams and Fraud

Scams are everywhere, especially online. Scammers often target teens because they may not know what to watch out for.

Whether it's a fake online store or a text message that says you've won a prize, scams can quickly drain your money and leave you feeling frustrated.

How to Spot a Scam

- **Too Good to Be True**: If someone offers you a way to make a lot of money quickly and easily, it's probably a scam. Legitimate opportunities usually need time, effort, and often some initial investment.

- **Suspicious Links**: Be careful about clicking on links in emails, texts, or social media messages from people you don't know. These links may lead to phishing sites designed to steal your personal information or infect your device with malware.

- **Requests for Personal Information**: Never give out your bank account details, Social Security number, or credit card information to someone you don't trust. Legitimate organizations will never ask for this sensitive information via unsecured channels like email or text messages.

Example: You get a message saying you've won a free gift card, but you need to pay a small fee to claim it. This is a common scam.

If it were really free, you wouldn't need to pay anything.

How to Avoid Scams

- **Do Your Research**: Look up reviews of a website or company before making a purchase. Check for customer feedback, ratings on trusted review sites, and any news articles about the company's reputation.
- **Ask an Adult**: If something doesn't seem right, check with a trusted adult before giving out any information. They may have more experience in spotting scams and can offer valuable advice.
- **Use Secure Payment Methods**: Pay with a credit card or a secure online payment system like PayPal. Avoid sending money directly or using wire transfers.

These secure methods often offer buyer protection and can help you recover funds if you fall victim to a scam.

Pitfall 3: Not Having an Emergency Fund

An emergency fund is a small savings account you can use for unexpected expenses, like a broken phone or an urgent trip. Many teens don't think they need one, but having a little money set aside can be a lifesaver.

Example: Your bike gets a flat tire on your way to school, and you need $20 for repairs. Without an emergency fund, you might have to borrow money from a friend or parent.

With an emergency fund, you can cover the cost and pay yourself back later.

How to Build an Emergency Fund

- **Start Small**: Aim for $100 to $200 to start. You can add to it over time. Even small contributions can add up and provide a financial cushion when unexpected expenses arise.
- **Save Automatically**: Set up a transfer from your checking account to your savings account every time you get paid. This "pay yourself first" approach ensures you're consistently building your emergency fund without having to think about it.
- **Only Use It for Emergencies**: Don't dip into your emergency fund for regular expenses or non-urgent purchases. Define what forms an emergency for you and stick to those guidelines to maintain the integrity of your fund.

Pitfall 4: Overspending on Credit Cards

Credit cards can be useful, but they're also one of the easiest ways to get into debt. It's tempting to use a credit card for things you can't afford, but this can lead to a cycle of debt that's hard to escape.

Example: You use a credit card to buy $300 worth of clothes, thinking you'll pay it off next month. But when the bill comes, you only have enough to make the minimum payment.

Now you're stuck paying interest, and it will take longer to pay off the balance.

How to Avoid Credit Card Debt

- **Only Charge What You Can Pay Off**: If you can't afford to pay for something in cash, don't put it on your credit card. This rule helps confirm you're not spending beyond your means and accumulating debt.

- **Pay Your Balance in Full**: Always aim to pay off your entire balance each month to avoid interest charges. This practice helps you maintain a good credit score and avoid costly interest payments.

- **Set a Spending Limit**: Decide how much you'll allow yourself to charge each month and stick to it. This self-imposed limit can help you stay within your budget and avoid overspending.

Pitfall 5: Not Tracking Your Spending

It's easy to lose track of where your money goes if you don't write it down or use a budgeting app. Small purchases, like snacks and drinks, can add up without you realizing it.

Example: You spend $5 a day on coffee. That doesn't seem like much, but over a month, that's $150! By cutting back, you could save a lot of money.

How to Track Your Spending

- **Use a Budgeting App**: There are many free apps that help you track your income and expenses. These apps can categorize your spending, set budget limits, and provide visual representations of your financial habits.

- **Write It Down**: Keep a notebook or a note on your phone where you record everything you spend. This manual method can make you more aware of each purchase and help you identify areas where you might be overspending.

- **Review Weekly**: Take a few minutes at the end of each week to see where your money went and if you need to make any changes. This regular review helps you stay on top of your finances and make adjustments to your spending habits as needed.

Practical Exercise: Identify Your Own Financial Pitfall

Think about your own spending habits. Are there areas where you tend to overspend or make impulse purchases?

Write down one mistake you've made before and a plan for how you'll avoid it in the future.

Example:

- **Mistake**: I spend too much on takeout food.

- **Plan**: I will limit myself to one takeout meal per week and cook at home more often.

To achieve this, I'll plan my meals in advance, learn some simple recipes, and set a specific budget for groceries and eating out.

Final Thoughts on Avoiding Money Mistakes

Everyone makes financial mistakes at some point, and that's okay. The key is to learn from them and make changes so you don't keep repeating them.

By being aware of these common pitfalls, problems, issues, problems, issues and having a plan in place, you're already ahead of the game.

In the next chapter, we're going to shift gears and talk about the importance of giving back. You'll learn how sharing your wealth, even in small amounts, can make a big impact on your life and the lives of others.

Ready to explore the power of generosity?

8. Giving Back: The Joy of Philanthropy and Sharing Wealth

We've spent a lot of time talking about how to earn, save, and grow your money. But there's another important aspect of building wealth that we need to discuss: **Giving back (philanthropy)**.

You might be thinking, "Wait, I'm just learning how to manage my money – why should I give it away?" Here's the secret: sharing your wealth, even in small amounts, can be one of the most rewarding things you can do.

It feels amazing to help others, and it can actually make you feel richer in the process.

Why Giving Back Matters

Giving back isn't about donating money to charity. It's about using your resources – time, skills, and money – to make a positive impact on the world.

Here's why it's important:

- **It Makes You Happier**: Studies show that people who give back are often happier and more satisfied with their lives. This is because giving activates the pleasure centers in our brain, releasing endorphins that create a positive feeling often referred to as a "helper's high."

- **It Helps Build a Better World**: Even small acts of kindness can make a big difference in someone else's life. When we contribute to improving our community or supporting a cause, we're actively participating in creating positive change, which can have far-reaching effects beyond what we initially see.

- **It's Part of Financial Health**: True wealth isn't about having money - this involves using it wisely and helping others along the way. Incorporating giving into your financial plan can help you develop a more balanced and fulfilling relationship with money.

Think about this: If you have $10 and you give $1 to someone who really needs it, you've just made a big impact on their day without losing much yourself. It's a win-win!

This concept illustrates how even small contributions can have a significant impact, especially when the recipient is in great need.

Different Ways to Give Back

There are many ways to give back, and it doesn't always have to involve money. Here are some ideas:

1. Donate Money

If you have extra cash, consider donating to a charity or cause you care about. Even small amounts can help.

- **Choose a Cause You Care About**: What matters to you? Animals? The environment? Helping kids in need? Find a charity that aligns with your values. This personal connection will make your giving more meaningful and sustainable in the long run.

- **Set a Giving Goal**: Just like you set savings goals, set a goal for how much you want to give back each month or year. This helps make giving a consistent part of your financial plan rather than an afterthought.

Example: If you set aside just $5 a month for donations, that's $60 a year. It might not seem like much, but it can buy food for a shelter animal or help a child get school supplies.

To put this in perspective, $60 could provide a week's worth of meals for a family in need or purchase several textbooks for underprivileged students.

2. Volunteer Your Time

Donating your time can be just as valuable as giving money. Plus, it's a great way to meet new people and learn new skills.

- **Find Local Opportunities**: Look for volunteer opportunities in your community, like helping at a food bank, animal shelter, or community cleanup event. These activities help others and give you a chance to connect with your local community and understand it's needs better.

- **Use Your Skills**: Are you good at tutoring? Offer to help a younger student with their homework.

Enjoy baking? Make treats for a fundraiser. By leveraging your unique talents, you can provide specialized help that might be particularly valuable to certain organizations or people.

Example: If you love animals, volunteer at a local shelter. You get to spend time with cute pets and help them find homes – a win for everyone!

This could involve tasks like walking dogs, socializing cats, or helping with adoption events, all of which contribute to the well-being of animals and increase their chances of finding forever homes.

3. Support a Friend in Need

Giving back doesn't always have to be through a charity. Sometimes, the best way to help is to support someone close to you who's going through a tough time.

- **Offer to Help**: If a friend is struggling, ask how you can help. It could be as simple as buying them lunch or helping them study for a big test.

Sometimes, just being there to listen can be incredibly valuable.

- **Share What You Have**: Do you have extra clothes, books, or supplies you don't need? Consider giving them to someone who could use them. This helps others and promotes sustainability by reducing waste.

Tip: Acts of kindness don't have to be big to make an impact. Even something small, like buying a coffee for a friend who's having a bad day, can make a difference.

These small gestures can brighten someone's day and strengthen your relationships.

How Giving Back Can Help You Grow

Giving isn't just good for the person receiving help - it's also good for you. Here's how:

- **Builds Gratitude**: When you give back, you appreciate what you have even more. Helping those in need can provide perspective on your own life and circumstances, fostering a sense of gratitude for what you have.

- **Teaches Responsibility**: It helps you think about how to use your money and time wisely. By incorporating giving into your financial plan, you learn to balance different priorities and make conscious decisions about resource allocation.

- **Creates Connections**: Volunteering and helping others can introduce you to new people and communities. These connections can broaden your perspective, provide networking opportunities, and even lead to new friendships or mentorship relationships.

Fun Fact: Many successful people, like Bill Gates and Oprah Winfrey, are big philanthropists. They believe that sharing their wealth is one of the keys to their happiness and success.

These people often credit their philanthropic efforts with giving them a sense of purpose beyond their business achievements.

Making Giving Part of Your Financial Plan

Just like you budget for savings and expenses, you can also budget for giving. Here's how:

1. **Decide How Much to Give**: It doesn't have to be a lot. Even 1% to 5% of your income can make a difference. Start small and increase your giving as your financial situation improves.

2. **Choose Where to Give**: Pick a charity, organization, or cause that you're passionate about. Research the organization to ensure your donation will be used effectively.

3. **Set a Regular Giving Schedule**: Make it a habit to give back regularly, whether it's monthly or a few times a year. Consistency in giving can help organizations plan their activities and budgets more effectively.

Example: If you earn $200 a month from a part-time job, setting aside just $5 for donations can go a long way. You can donate it to a charity or use it to help someone in your community.

This $5 could provide a meal for a homeless person, contribute to school supplies for a child in need, or support conservation efforts for endangered species.

Practical Exercise: Create a Giving Plan

Let's put what you've learned into action. Create a simple plan for how you want to give back this month.

1. **Choose a Way to Give:** Will you donate money, volunteer your time, or help a friend in need? Consider your current resources and commitments when making this decision.

2. **Set a Goal**: How much time or money will you give? (e.g., "I will donate $10 to a local food bank this month" or "I will volunteer for 2 hours at the animal shelter next weekend.") Make sure your goal is specific, measurable, and achievable.

3. **Make It Happen**: Follow through with your plan and see how it feels to make a difference. Reflect on the experience and how it impacts both you and the recipient of your generosity.

The Ripple Effect of Kindness

When you give back, you create a ripple effect of kindness. Your small act of generosity can inspire others to do the same, creating a chain reaction that spreads positivity and goodwill.

It's amazing to think that your actions, no matter how small, can have a big impact on the world.

Example: You donate $10 to a fundraiser for clean water. That money helps build a well in a village that didn't have clean water before.

Now, the people in that village are healthier and can focus on building their community.

Your small donation helped make that possible! This example illustrates how a seemingly small contribution can lead to significant improvements in people's lives, affecting not just people but entire communities.

Final Thoughts on Giving Back

Giving back is one of the most powerful things you can do with your money and time. It reminds us that wealth isn't about having a lot of money – this involves using what we have to make the world a better place.

By including giving in your financial plan, you're helping others, but you're also becoming a more generous and fulfilled person.

In the next chapter, we're going to pull everything together and help you create your very own financial plan. You'll learn how to put all these skills into action and build a roadmap for your financial future.

Ready to take the final step?

9. Creating Your Personal Financial Plan: A Roadmap to Wealth

Alright, budgeting is cool, and by now, you've got that part down. **But let's think bigger—like way bigger.**

What if you had a plan for your money that didn't just help you get through the month, but could actually shape your future? That's what a **Personal Financial Plan** is all about.

This is not about tracking your spending (been there, done that). A financial plan is like your personal map for life—it helps you figure out where you want to go and how you're going to get there. Whether you dream of buying your first car, traveling the world, or even starting your own business, your financial plan is the roadmap that gets you there.

Let's dive in and create your own **roadmap to wealth**!

What Even Is a Financial Plan?

Okay, so you've heard of budgets (thanks, Chapter 2). A financial plan is like a next-level budget—it's not just about how you spend or save this month - this involves your whole life.

Think of it as your money game plan. It's the strategy for:

- **What you want to do with your money** (goals)
- **How you're going to make it happen** (actions)
- **How to handle the unexpected** (a safety net)

In other words, this involves making sure your money works for you—not the other way around.

A financial plan goes beyond just allocating your current income. It involves setting long-term goals, creating strategies to achieve those goals, and adjusting your approach as circumstances change.

Why Bother with a Financial Plan?

Here's the deal: life is full of choices. A financial plan helps you make smarter ones.

When you have a plan, you can:

- **Save for the cool stuff**: Want to buy a car? Save for college? It's all possible with a plan.
- **Stress less**: You know you've got your money under control.
- **Grow your money**: Saving is awesome, but investing? That's where the magic happens.

Bottom line: A financial plan helps you live the life you want, not just the life you can afford *right now*.

Having a financial plan provides a framework for making informed decisions about your money. It allows you to prioritize your spending and saving based on what's truly important to you, rather than making impulsive choices.

This structured approach can lead to greater financial security and the ability to achieve your goals faster.

How to Build Your Financial Plan (Without Losing Your Mind)

We're keeping this simple, step-by-step style—just like building your first budget. Let's break it down.

Step 1: Dream Big and Set Your Goals

First up: What do you actually want out of life? Think about the short-term (the next year or two), medium-term (3–5 years), and long-term (5+ years).

Here are some examples:

- **Short-term goals**: Save $1,000 for a new phone or laptop.
- **Medium-term goals**: Buy your first car, travel with friends, or build an emergency fund.
- **Long-term goals**: Save for college, start a business, or invest for the future.

Tip: Be specific. "Save for a car" is good, but "Save $5,000 for a used car in 3 years" is way better. Why? Because now you know *exactly* what you're working toward.

Setting specific goals is crucial because it allows you to create a clear action plan. When you have a precise target, you can break it down into smaller, manageable steps. This makes your goals feel more achievable and helps you track your progress more effectively. Specific goals also help you stay motivated because you can see your advancement towards a concrete objective.

Step 2: Check Your Starting Line

Before you can plan your money's future, figure out where it's at *right now*. Write down:

- **Your income**: All the money you get from jobs, allowances, or side hustles.
- **Your savings**: How much you already have saved.
- **Your spending**: Where your money goes every month.

This is like taking a snapshot of your money life. Once you know where you stand, it's easier to figure out your next move.

Understanding your current financial situation is essential because it provides a realistic foundation for your plan. Knowing your income helps you decide how much you can allocate towards your goals.

Assessing your savings gives you an idea of your financial cushion and how close you are to your targets.

Analyzing your spending patterns reveals areas where you might be able to cut back and redirect money towards your goals.

Step 3: Make a Game Plan for Your Goals

Now that you've got your goals and know where you're starting from, it's time to connect the dots. Here's how:

1. **Figure out how much you need**: Break each goal into a dollar amount and a deadline. Example: Need $1,200 for a laptop in a year? That's $100/month.

2. **Adjust your budget**: Look at your spending and find ways to save for your goals. Maybe you cut back on snacks or skip some impulse buys to save more.

3. **Automate it**: Set up a system to make saving easy. Use apps or automatic bank transfers to stash money before you're tempted to spend it.

Tip: Start with one goal at a time. Once you crush that, move on to the next!

Breaking down your goals into specific dollar amounts and deadlines makes them more tangible and achievable. This approach allows you to create a concrete savings plan.

Adjusting your budget to accommodate these goals confirms that you're actively working towards them rather than just hoping to have enough money left over at the end of the month.

Automation is powerful because it removes the temptation to spend the money elsewhere and makes saving a habit rather than a conscious decision each time.

Step 4: Build a "What-If" Fund

Life happens, and sometimes, it's not great. That's why you need an **emergency fund**—money you set aside for when things go wrong, like unexpected expenses or a loss of income.

How much should you save? Aim for 3–6 months of basic expenses.

Don't worry if that feels huge—it's okay to start small. Even $10 a week adds up over time.

An emergency fund is crucial because it provides a financial buffer against unexpected events. Without it, you might be forced to rely on high-interest credit cards or loans when emergencies arise, which can derail your financial progress.

The 3-6 month guideline is based on the average time it might take to find new employment or recover from a financial setback.

Starting small and building up over time makes this goal more achievable and helps you develop a saving habit.

Step 5: Think Bigger with Investing

Saving is awesome, but if you really want to grow your money, you need to look into **investing**. Before you freak out, here's the deal: investing doesn't have to be scary or complicated.

Start small with:

- **Index funds**: These are like a bundle of stocks you can buy all at once.
- **ETFs (Exchange-Traded Funds)**: Similar to index funds,

but even easier for beginners.

- **Robo-advisors**: Apps that handle investments for you.

Why invest? Because of something called compound growth. Basically, your money earns money, and then that money earns money, and so on. It's like planting a money tree—start early, and it grows way bigger.

Investing is important because it allows your money to grow faster than inflation, which is the general increase in prices over time. While savings accounts offer security, their interest rates often don't keep pace with inflation, meaning your money could lose purchasing power over time.

Index funds and ETFs offer diversification, spreading your risk across many companies or sectors.

Robo-advisors use algorithms to create and manage a diversified portfolio based on your risk tolerance and goals, making investing more accessible to beginners.

Compound growth is powerful because it speeds up your money's growth over time. For example, if you invest $1,000 and earn a 7% annual return, after 10 years you'd have about $1,967. But after 30 years, you'd have about $7,612 – all from that initial $1,000 investment.

This is why starting to invest early, even with small amounts, can lead to significant wealth accumulation over time.

Keeping Your Plan on Track

A financial plan isn't "set it and forget it." You've got to check in regularly and make adjustments as needed. Here's how:

- **Review every month**: Did you save as much as you planned? Did you overspend anywhere?

- **Make changes**: If your goals or income change, update your plan.
- **Celebrate your wins**: Hit a savings goal? Treat yourself to something small—it's all about balance.

Regular reviews are essential because they help you stay accountable and ensure you're making progress towards your goals. They also allow you to identify and address any issues quickly before they become major problems.

Life circumstances and financial situations can change, so being flexible and willing to adjust your plan is crucial for long-term success.

Celebrating small wins helps maintain motivation and reinforces positive financial behaviors.

Why Your Plan Is Your Superpower

Here's the cool thing: most people don't have a financial plan. They're just winging it and hoping for the best. But not you.

You're building something amazing—a roadmap to your dreams. That's a superpower if I've ever seen one.

So, grab a notebook, sketch out your goals, and start building your plan. You've got this—and your future self will thank you.

Having a financial plan sets you apart because it gives you direction and purpose for your money. It allows you to make intentional choices rather than reactive ones, which can lead to better financial outcomes over time.

Your plan also provides a framework for handling financial challenges and opportunities, giving you greater confidence and control over your financial life.

10. Your Journey to Financial Independence Starts Now

Woohoo! You've made it to the final chapter of the book.

By now, you've learned how to set financial goals, budget your money, save effectively, invest wisely, build good credit, avoid common pitfalls, problems, issues, and even give back to your community.

You've gained a set of skills that many adults are still trying to master. So, what's next?

It's time to put everything you've learned into action and start your path toward financial independence.

What Is Financial Independence?

Financial independence means having enough money to support yourself without relying on others. It's the freedom to make choices about your life without worrying about money.

It doesn't mean you have to be super rich - it just means that you have control over your finances and can live comfortably without stress.

Financial independence provides you with the ability to make decisions based on your personal goals and values, as opposed to being constrained by financial limitations. This could include choosing a career you're passionate about, even if it's not the highest-paying option, or having the flexibility to take time off work to pursue personal interests or further education.

Imagine This: You want to take a trip with your friends next summer. Because you've been budgeting, saving, and investing, you have the money to pay for it without going into debt or asking your parents for help.

That's financial independence in action!

The Keys to Achieving Financial Independence

Achieving financial independence doesn't happen overnight. It takes time, patience, and a commitment to building good habits.

Here are the key steps you need to follow:

1. Keep Setting New Goals

Setting goals isn't something you do just once. As you achieve your goals, it's important to set new ones.

This helps you stay focused and motivated.

Goal-setting is an ongoing process that allows you to continually challenge yourself and grow financially. As you reach one milestone, setting a new, more ambitious goal keeps you moving forward on your financial journey.

This could mean increasing your savings rate, targeting a higher investment return, or planning for larger purchases or life events.

Tip: Review your goals every few months and update them as needed. If you've reached a savings goal, set a new one that's a bit more challenging.

For example, if you've successfully saved $500, your next goal might be to save $1,000 or to invest a portion of your savings.

2. Stick to Your Budget

Your budget is your financial blueprint. It shows you where your money is going and helps you make smart decisions.

Make sure you review your budget regularly and adjust it if your income or expenses change.

A budget is not a static document - it should evolve as your financial situation changes. Regular reviews confirm that your budget stays an accurate reflection of your financial reality.

This might involve adjusting spending categories, accounting for changes in income, or reallocating funds as your priorities shift.

Tip: Use a budgeting app to track your spending and stay on top of your finances. The more you use your budget, the easier it will become.

Many apps offer features like automatic categorization of expenses, visual representations of your spending patterns, and alerts when you're approaching budget limits in certain categories.

3. Build Your Savings and Emergency Fund

Continue adding to your savings and building your emergency fund. Aim to have at least three to six months' worth of expenses saved in your emergency fund as you get older.

This will give you a financial cushion in case something unexpected happens.

An emergency fund is crucial for financial stability. It provides a safety net that can help you avoid going into debt when unexpected expenses arise.

These could include medical bills, car repairs, or covering living expenses if you lose your job.

By having this fund, you can handle financial surprises without derailing your long-term financial plans.

Exercise: Set a new savings goal for your emergency fund. How much do you want to save, and by when?

Write it down and create a plan to reach it.

For instance, if you want to save $1,000 in six months, you'd need to set aside about $167 per month. Break this down further into weekly or bi-weekly savings targets to make it more manageable.

4. Invest Consistently

Investing is one of the greatest tools for building wealth. Even if you can only invest small amounts, do it consistently.

The earlier you start, the more time your money has to grow.

Consistent investing allows you to take advantage of dollar-cost averaging, which means you buy more shares when prices are low and fewer when prices are high. This strategy can help reduce the impact of market volatility on your investments over time.

Additionally, starting early gives your investments more time to benefit from compound interest, where you earn returns not just on your initial investment, and on the returns from previous years.

Example: If you invest $50 a month in an ETF with an average annual return of 8%, you could have over $36,000 in 20 years. The key is to start early and stay consistent.

This example shows the power of compound interest and regular investing.

Even small amounts can grow significantly over time when invested consistently.

5. Avoid Debt and Use Credit Wisely

Debt can be a major obstacle on your path to financial independence. Be careful with credit cards and loans, and always pay off your balances in full if possible.

If you do need to take on debt (like for college), make a plan to pay it off as quickly as you can.

While some debt, like student loans or a mortgage, can be considered "good debt" because they invest in your future or in an appreciating asset, high-interest consumer debt can significantly hinder your financial progress. Credit card debt, in particular, can accumulate quickly due to high interest rates, making it difficult to pay off and potentially damaging your credit score.

Tip: Set a rule for yourself: Only use your credit card for planned purchases, and never charge more than you can afford to pay off each month. This approach helps you build a good credit history without falling into debt.

Consider setting up automatic payments for the full balance each month to confirm you never miss a payment.

Mindset Matters: Think Like a Wealth Builder

Your mindset plays a big role in your financial success. If you think of yourself as a wealth builder and make decisions with your long-term goals in mind, you'll be much more likely to achieve financial independence.

Developing a wealth-building mindset involves shifting your perspective from short-term gratification to long-term financial security. This means prioritizing saving and investing over unnecessary spending, viewing setbacks as learning opportunities as opposed to failures, and consistently educating yourself about personal finance and investment strategies.

- **Be Patient:** Building wealth takes time. Don't get discouraged if you don't see big results right away.

Remember that compound interest works best over long periods, and consistent small actions can lead to significant results over time.

- **Stay Positive:** Focus on your progress, not your setbacks. Every small step you take is bringing you closer to your goals.

Celebrate your financial wins, no matter how small, as they reinforce positive financial behaviors.

- **Keep Learning:** The financial world is always changing. Keep learning about new strategies, tools, and opportunities to grow your wealth.

This could involve reading financial books, following reputable financial blogs, or even taking online courses in personal finance or investing.

Quote to Remember: "The best time to plant a tree was 20 years ago. The second best time is now." – Chinese Proverb

This proverb emphasizes that while it's ideal to start early, it's never too late to begin your financial journey. The most important thing is to start taking action now, regardless of your current age or financial situation.

Practical Exercise: Create Your Vision Board

A vision board is a fun way to visualize your financial goals and dreams. It's a collage of pictures, quotes, and words that represent what you want to achieve.

Creating a vision board helps make your financial goals more tangible and can serve as a powerful motivational tool. By visually representing your goals, you create a constant reminder of what you're working towards, which can help you stay focused and motivated, especially during challenging times.

How to Create a Vision Board:

1. Get a piece of paper, poster board, or open a digital app like Canva.

2. Find pictures and quotes that represent your goals (e.g., a picture of a car you want to buy, a quote about saving, or an image of a vacation spot you want to visit).
3. Arrange the pictures and quotes on your board and place it somewhere you'll see it every day.

When selecting images and quotes for your vision board, choose ones that genuinely resonate with you and align with your personal financial goals. The more meaningful and personal your vision board is, the more effective it will be in motivating you.

Tip: Use your vision board as a daily reminder of why you're working hard to manage your money. It will help keep you motivated and focused on your goals.

Consider taking a photo of your vision board and setting it as your phone or computer wallpaper for an additional daily reminder.

Your friends might start asking you for money tips. Your family might notice your smart decisions.

You could inspire others to start their own financial journeys.

Financial literacy and responsible money management are skills that can positively impact entire communities. As you become more financially savvy, you may find opportunities to share your knowledge with others, contributing to improved financial well-being for those around you.

Example: You help a friend set up their first budget. They start saving money, reach their goals, and feel more confident about their finances.

Your decision to take charge of your money has created a positive ripple effect that spreads to the people around you.

This example illustrates how your financial knowledge can benefit others. As your friend experiences success with budgeting, they may be inspired to learn more about personal finance and share their experiences with others, further extending the positive impact.

Your Next Steps: Take Action Today

You've learned a lot in this book, but knowledge is only powerful if you use it. Here are some actions you can take right now to get started on your path to financial independence:

1. **Review Your Goals:** Look back at the financial goals you set earlier in the book. Are they still relevant? Do you need to make any changes? Consider how your circumstances or priorities may have shifted since you initially set these goals, and adjust them accordingly.

2. **Check Your Budget:** Review your budget and make sure it reflects your current income and expenses. Adjust it if needed. This might involve updating income figures, reassessing spending categories, or reallocating funds based on your current priorities.

3. **Make a Savings Deposit:** Put some money into your savings account or emergency fund today, even if it's just a small amount. This action reinforces the habit of saving and gets you one step closer to your financial goals.

4. **Invest for Your Future:** If you haven't started investing yet, make a plan to begin. Even $10 can be a good start. Research different investment options that align with your goals and risk tolerance, and consider setting up automatic

investments to make the process easier.

5. **Share What You've Learned:** Tell a friend or family member about one thing you learned from this book. Teaching others will help reinforce your own knowledge. This could involve explaining a concept, sharing a tip, or discussing how you've applied what you've learned to your own finances.

Final Words: You've Got This!

The fact that you're reading this book and learning about money management at a young age already puts you ahead of the game. You've taken the time to learn important skills that will help you make smart financial decisions and build a bright future.

Financial independence is a journey, not a destination.

There will be ups and downs along the way, but every step you take is bringing you closer to your goals.

You have the tools, the knowledge, and the mindset to succeed. So go out there, take control of your finances, and start building the life you've always dreamed of.

Your future self will thank you for it.

You're Ready – Now It's Time to Take Action!

Go back through the exercises and activities in this book. Pick one thing you can start working on today, whether it's setting a new goal, creating a budget, or making your first investment.

The most important step is the first one – and you've already taken it by reading this book.

Remember that financial management is an ongoing process. It's okay to make mistakes along the way – what's important is that you learn from them and keep moving forward.

Don't be afraid to ask for help or seek out additional resources if you need them.

Congratulations on finishing *10 Money Skills For Teenagers: Your Superpower To Create Wealth*! Your pathway is just beginning, and the possibilities are endless. Remember, every page you read and every concept you grasp is an investment in yourself and a significant step towards financial independence and success.

YOU! Yes YOU!, have the power to shape your own financial future, so why not get started TODAY!

***

A Note of Appreciation

To my incredible readers,

Thanks for picking up ***10 Money Skills for Teenagers: Your Superpower to Create Wealth,*** I really appreciate it. Could I ask you to please leave me a review on Amazon. It goes a long way to making sure other teens like yourself benefit from what you have learned.

If you're looking for even more advice on growing your independence and building a strong foundation for the future, check out my other teen books:

1. ***Life Skills for the Teenage Soul: The Ultimate Guide to Building Resilience and Independence.*** It's packed with insights on understanding yourself, building strong relationships, managing stress, surviving high school and planning a successful, healthy future. Think of it as your go-to guide for figuring out the real-life stuff nobody teaches in school. Grab it at **https://mybook.to/Life-skills-teens**

2. ***100 Practical Skills for Teenagers: The Ultimate Guide For Everday Challenges*** - From simple meal prep to changing a tire, to DIY skills to basic first aid, this book is packed with tips and hacks designed to help you tackle the real-life stuff and feel more confident. Grab it at **https://mybook.to/practical-skills-teens**

With heartfelt thanks,
Elizabeth E James
https://amazon.com/author/elizabethejames

Made in the USA
Monee, IL
04 November 2026

67379932R00056